WILD CURIOUS AIR

By the same author

A History Of What I'll Become
Viva The Real
Brink
The Quality of Light and other poems (chapbook)
The Leaves Are My Sisters (chapbook)
Breaking the Days
The Beautiful Anxiety
Ash is Here, So are Stars
Dark Bright Doors
Senses Working Out (chapbook)
Speak Which: Hay(na)ku Poems (chapbook)
Broken/Open
Fold Unfold (chapbook)
Struggle and Radiance: Ten Commentaries (chapbook)
Where the Sea Burns (chapbook)
Screens Jets Heaven: New and Selected Poems
The Book of Possibilities
Flagging Down Time
The Mask and the Jagged Star

WILD CURIOUS AIR

JILL JONES

RECENT
WORK
PRESS

Wild Curious Air
Recent Work Press
Canberra, Australia

Copyright © Jill Jones, 2020

ISBN: 9780648834342 (paperback)

 A catalogue record for this book is available from the National Library of Australia

All rights reserved. This book is copyright. Except for private study, research, criticism or reviews as permitted under the Copyright Act, no part of this book may be reproduced, stored in a retrieval system, or transmitted in any form by any means without prior written permission. Enquiries should be addressed to the publisher.

Cover image: 'Clouds Fill Windows and Skies Look On',
 © Annette Willis, 2020. Reproduced with permission.
Cover design: Recent Work Press
Set by Recent Work Press

recentworkpress.com

SS

For Annette

'Hold my hand when it gets even scarier'

I pay my respects to the Kaurna people, the traditional custodians and songmakers of the country where most of these poems were written and where this manuscript was put together, and to their elders, past, present and emerging. Sovereignty was never ceded.

Contents

Deliberation on Sudden Days of Exceptional Brightness	1
Time Would Choose	2
Out of These Curves	3
Everything Hurts	4
At an Hour Like Death	5
The Moon, Antares, and the Dead As Well	6
I Walk As Jittery Mortal	8
'It doesn't hurt to fall off the moon'	9
Possible Manners Of Revelation	10
Falling Shadows, Dizzy Seed, Changing Each Memory Song	12
Sometimes an Ant	15
A Tally of Desire	16
Last Small Things	17
In Dark-dreamt / And Morning / Come / Gather	18
The Cure	20
Standing Under	21
Why The Gods Are Not Our Friends	22
I Welcome Night's Ruins	25
A Piece of Everything	26
The Vertigo Blues	27
Unhappy Fortune	28
Day Shifts	31
To enter / As you enter / Entrances	32
Light Falling West	35
Symposium of the Unfinished	36
Between Here and the Underworld	40
Still, Life	42
Everything comes – at first glance	43
'I only wanted to see what the garden was like'	44
I'm Almost Good	46
Here We Are	48
Future Shadow	49
Dark Heart	57

Darling Sense	58
Undo Everything	60
Wild Curious Air	62
Afterword	63

Deliberation on Sudden Days of Exceptional Brightness

These were the lines of our life here
along the street. Cars were all candid
in their leaving. No-one could make a decision.
We meditated on timetables. We thought
about spending wisely, messaging coupons.
We became aware of sirens and strangers
of early flights, all but solitude.

Thought had drugged the music. It was
reduced to interest rates, beautiful soft furnishings
on night programs. Despite the poster's
green outline, it was old politics, tea cups,
amiable kickbacks. Doors closed. There were
only clicks. Poets made words of little boats.
The air could not be still.

Yet, how sanguine the rain became between
the lightning. The sky rhymed with
747s, Cessnas, drones. We were still there
washed in discordant fashion sense.
There was a gulf that didn't allow sleep.
Choices were wrapped in colours of the same size.
It was clear at this stage but inevitably failing.

There were also exceptional bright days
almost as if weather could no longer alarm us.
It was not the time to hate everything.
But not quite the time to dance. We gave up
determining fences. We'd ask, who is my enemy?
Or post, 'Do not abandon these words.'
As if that was the answer.

Time Would Choose

What is the magpie searching for next to the path
All this summer we've felt only dust
A tree has fallen, its sap taken by drought's gravity
its smash of branches like a burst moon

I trace ancient blur in the floating night
those tiny points spilling from the galaxy's breast
The creek is torpid and smells like a sour sea
The bushlands seem to crackle and splinter like bones

I can tell myself its natural that everything dies
But when is death a place or time you would choose
to lie down together with the soil and the stone
to give up the air and the song in your mouth

Rather be with sky, or with the magpie and dust
Rather be vagrant than something you'd own

Out of These Curves

Each building looks like a letter bending the frame.
It's easy to hide in the curves
where water drips like a song.

The list we kept of daily rainfall had a lot of zeroes.
It's harder to read the sunlight between
hunched floors of the car park.

See this backpack leaning against the wall.
Perhaps it's lost.
Those high ledges give me the blues.

On the bus I concentrate on Dickinson's dashes
and Keats' bad spelling. Sometimes I feel
exiled from my language as if avoiding road works.

Sky's beautiful dry shadows fall on my pages
through the familiar spectrum.
All my food's been wrapped in words.

I'm talking with a corrupted document file,
old notes, the spreadsheet I thought I'd lost.
Perpendiculars aren't comforting.

The book I intended to finish is still at home
on the bedside table. Tonight rare rain will drip
like a meticulous dream into the roof cavity.

There's a soft insistent sound in the grevilleas.
Even the yellow door is sighing.
I'm still forming words out of these curves.

Everything Hurts

Animals try to hide from the gaze, and the light
People run around with nets and syringes

The voiceovers mean things are hidden
The filming is secretive

It seems important and inhumane
Everything hurts — so, maybe that's the case

Things are not so much objects
Maybe they will simplify or die

Besides, what breath creates light each day
On what surfaces does the wind blow

There's mist over the trees
There's no comfort, as if there ever was

But I still have fur and skin
which seems painful, pretentious and fabulously stupid

At an Hour Like Death

The hasps slip off
   the morning.
It's as though a vault
     renounces its estate.
There's a new opera of flash, then
   moss and phosphorous.

The moments blanch
    in the molten pane.
It's not a prank this time.
    That's an older lexicon
      the teasing charter of memories
now dimly presumptuous.

Here's a more sober truth.
And yet it fumbles still
   in a pocket.
What could it extract?
Figments, balms
   a breeze.

Something of magnitude
    the calyx, the butterfly, a crowd
     a gulf to cross.

Plummetless dawn.

The Moon, Antares, and the Dead As Well

'The problem of time is like the darkness of the sky'

—*John Berger*

We don't see our faces in the stars, tonight, or any night.
   They're older than faces.
What do we do with the problem of time? I wonder what rivers do.
   Or estuaries, atoms, clouds, constellations, in their time.
All those traces as threads, so even the absent are present.
   The dead as well.
As though there's a perimeter, an edge to the realm-that's-not-us.

Look, there's the past, the crescent moon! And above it Venus
   then Jupiter, and further up the sky, Antares in Scorpius.
The moon's light takes just over a second to reach our faces.
   That light from Antares left itself just before the birth of Galileo.
Always a past touches us, as this hot January forgets us.
   To imagine Galileo on such a night, as if he might
walk here still, looking for ancient heat above this heat.

This pulse of a big, old story is far from our traffic and trees,
   our ground's levels and hollows. We don't hear it.
We can only think and feel into this time, our time
   that remembers the living and 'all-that-the-living-are-not'.
But the dead aren't us.
   Nor are they stars, despite all the names up there.
Someone left a beer bottle next to the street tree.

I hear voices in a yard nearby.
   Who's speaking at this hour, charging the night?
Maybe in the dark, things are more tolerable.
   Maybe in the dark you're not yet born.
Tonight's cold thin moonlight falls onto their faces.
   Hear them laughing, not loudly.
Like a conspiracy. Of being with. Maybe together, outside.

Close your eyes and
  keep them open.
Maybe turned upwards into the past,
  or towards me now.
The past as now to come.
  Where we are also in past light
coming light.

I Walk As Jittery Mortal

I walk out into the curious air.
I trip on matter that's going cold.
I feel earth as thrust, metal and scrape.
I look at each plant for belief or breath.
Their brights unveil me as shadow or guest.

I want to feel a whole lot better than quiet.
I'm singing like a lost chorus of one.
Damp and grit play giddy round my shoes.
I step through it. Nothing quite catches.
Afternoon rain begins its restlessness.

Air is my home. I entered it dripping.
Now here's the jittery earth.
Now here's crust and brown flare
a muster of body for bodies.
Out here I hardly know myself, finally.

Sorrow isn't something I'd name.
It would only sound nostalgic or sappy.
This world isn't mine.
Here I'm a mortal subject.
There are cold things I can't brush away.

'It doesn't hurt to fall off the moon'

When night is naked,
it risks as much as us.
My mind spills like water.
You launch yourself into it.

Even while we're kidding around,
I unpack all your knots.
'What if we try this?'
What if we change each other.

Knots are possibilities. I weave them
out of themselves, tenderly,
curiously, like a charm,
or a plot difficult to relate.

How do women chase each other?
Teamwork, I guess, as we put each other
on, exchanging clothes neither of us
need. It becomes beautiful slapstick.

We fall into and out of each other
as reflections across a lake.
The night isn't tame or duplicitous.
We stroke and steer by the hours.

Your breath is my river.
I row with you into morning.

Possible Manners Of Revelation

I translate roses as multiples, a rose and a rose and a rose

I paint all my corners different colours

I welcome my own redundancies, and all that time to kill

I resurrect the dead for a second when I close my eyes

I slide that agnostic load from my shoulders in a flash of unearthing

I face east then west to respect my indirection

I swallow the moonlight and hope it may ward off the sincere and embarrassing shadows I've shed

I return to multiples

I alphabetise my dreams hoping for order

I set fire to my opinions and wait for the truce

I find lost amulets in the gutter left by cyclists or the stars and bless them again with unchained secrets

I strike light into the dark passage where the summer moths return

I forget my body is what I have with me until my fingers and breath do their work

I tinker with the time it takes to remember

I remember everyone I forgot

I promise the invisible I will return one day

I lean against the transcendent, listening to the honeyeaters fight in the camellias

I talk to absence like the one who has gone

I ask emptiness to fill me

I deface all my damage because the world won't forgive me

I recite a history of my own breath, which is the poem

Falling Shadows, Dizzy Seed, Changing Each Memory Song

1.

Moon time and bee time are different
and the same when your time's up

it's time for rain which is the veil
and also clarity through heat
sharing air with light

is this not an original art ever falling
as though repeating what can't be
repeated drop by drop

2.

Panes of winter
its skeletons
wet shiny shadows

bending blue
into each seam
of the world

from sky stacks
sewing weather

3.

Dizzy at night on the footpath, losing it, vertigo
Mirrors in the lift, something to avoid
The hours that never finish are also never still
At the entrance hard to enter
Verticals aren't easy

There's too much space on the page
Opened into spreading as a form of walking

The letter I never wrote

4.

as if there was more
space
in the continuum
for a song

whose chanting
sticks to you like a seed
using you to travel further than
you've ever been

5.

Can air be sweet?
It's not weightless.

Substance is distressed.
We are killers.

It is always dark
when the song's singing.

We're receding, not vanishing
and changing paradise.

6.

Who can say what each window on the square
could uncover or experience

What might be the attention of light

the push of summer, the extent of capital
arrangements of gods and choirs
a furore of government as if there were laws

As if what was grown stayed in place, as if
in each place, this could be said

7.

the natural state is
turning, there's no true
forecast without tomorrow's
work, the old dog scratches out
repetitions, an evening's
mote of dust now resides
in memory and the garden's
ferny root systems

8.

The newspaper spreads beyond the table
Shadows have their own colours
More hate speech

Is there some kind of process when crossing a line?

The announcements roll by too quickly
A red door is closing

The wall demands letters
Minutes drip like a song

Sometimes an Ant

Attention is a register as it dreams
   small dashes in the garden
streaks of moments in sunlight
    an economy of fragments
   gathered by time
speed as thrift and expansion

The day closes without
   the discretion
of an envelope
    speech still sounds
   and rattles among wood
and metal bitumen plastic leaf

Sometimes there's rain
   and that's
always brief
    nothing really closes over
   sentences and phrases
scattered through yards and streets

Sometimes an ant rolls a stone
   tiny dust is huge
or an equal task to the task of
    a bird splashing
   in a pool or an
ocean

A Tally of Desire

When stains are caresses
　When every preference is a debate or a need
Wishing to be astray
　'Not for the first time'
The appetite to go hither even if
　A stupor of rushed emptiness

Wanting to come in like a stranger
　When the wild space of afternoon doesn't pass
Gossiping at the fence as a scrap of paper floats by
　Each old object now strange
When my tongue breaks
　When reality lapses like a favour

When waking seems risky as sleep
　A trance state between season and accident
Being unable to speak
　The five ways night slows down
Even when asleep (especially then)
　Everything is tinged violet, every hollow

Zero as possibility　　an arrival

Last Small Things

Each day there's a dip in currency.
I hear that spike in reception.
We feel a tremor from a corrupted data file.
There's all those numb batteries.

I sit on a small piece of a large land
singing a song I still don't understand.
I feel small pustules on my skin
and rare rain that won't help me.

In the abandoned holiday cottage
I find a pile of dirty coal dust, scratched
gold medallions, an unfinished letter.
Near the wharf silvery fish scales collect.

I remember the taste of water from
a brass tap, the smell of flaking wallpaper.
I hear tidemarks rising, ice melting in a glass.
Here's a bottle of pills. The use-by dates.

In Dark-dreamt / And Morning / Come / Gather

     all last night in the dark-dreamt
nervy apparitions   draped in
telepathy   pale and cotton-neat
              outside scatters wake   asymmetric
              giddy pirouettes   not exactly real

someone races a car up and round
neighbourhood corners   as if
     somewhere to go   in speed
           hectoring and dilating the semantics
           for what might never

that what-every   jumpy and phantasmal
     (and yes again someone guns a car)
we forget   find one another
           knitted up in soft mechanics
           fur hand sinew   breast

we are branches too   we are swaying
           suppliants   covered in
           persuasions   our only place
and we come into the dark world   daily
    in body and dream of   the old body

    and for morning   come gather
nevertheless   the spoor of spring
           carry water into the wind-tampered
           unpicking the hard-sought
let garden heaviness gush   expectantly

while thought jumps   again
to praise   is another enough
garland hours   alone with all these others
          blossoms parrots   verses stones
               our feet in exuberant earth

The Cure

The Cool Moon

Things don't get any better
when they're getting worse.

It may be a truism
but so is the night
that sings like a blackbird
or something left on the moon.

All day I've tried to cool down.
It's not a cure but no-one else
seems to know what to do.

The Small Distancing

Let's stride out anyway
it's a lucky dip
like any day's weather
all over it the siren song
sparrow song

urban meadows old happy weeds
plush dwellings
and fancies in a yard
a tin roof patched for generations
for sale signs

plastic chimera   avian air

Standing Under

How it thins—
   autumn
     skin
       the social contract

Standing under a tree—
   the old nests
     frailty

Yet the ground
   this solid dust
packed into a star

Everyone wants you dead

   Who can avoid it
between
    this scratched earth
      the filthy sky—
wide
  older than

And still to come

Fuck you!
It's my death
  not yours

Why The Gods Are Not Our Friends

Once I was 18, and I still am
    but   my breath is waning   *à bout de souffle*
running in a field as if escaping
    or down a street towards the end.

At every cross road there's a god
    knowing we're all trying to escape
with the moon or summer days.

    It's not working, is it?

*

I wonder if the shades are writing.
If they've enrolled in a class of misty memoir.

    What would the gods know about poetry?

You invent things.
Let them go!

Language was always a mug's game.

*

What a friend we have in dust.
It's always there accompanying us.

Our destination, our reminder
taking up so little room
    underneath.

While all the medicines roll around
in bottles, in packets.

Perhaps that's the noise
which drives demons away.

*

The window is for far-seeing.
    And the sky at night even more.

My hand is for far-seeing.
    It's been in front of me all this time.

I know my hand like my hand.

I know the window and what it permits
    or assembles.

I can't see the wind. I can't see my mind.

I am alone   yet among   a great crowd.

*

They gave me a form—the gods.
    I wasn't sure how to fill it in.
They demanded an answer.
    I sent them a question—and an invoice.

They returned with a letter of demand.
    I'm not sure what letter it was.
Nothing from this alphabet
    but not magic either.

No-one paid up.

*

A wind blows through the house
    turning the air into a sea

The percussion of the banging blinds
    sets up a song in whispers and beats

Ravens gather in the old dead tree.

*

There's a skink in the bottom drawer

What's it living on?

I Welcome Night's Ruins

Night is the oldest of ruins I know.
But everything seems exact. I tell myself
there's no sin in looking backwards
if that's where the monsters went.

I listen for damage as something
crashes, is it a book or simply shapes
of things, a kind of blue after
midnight? A hundred translations.

The house itself isn't done or alone.
Where are all these extras? I remember
curtains but that doesn't help.
What sort of ghost do I prefer?

When I was born, night thought
about me, then later found me.
I'm still singing that song in the
thickets of its generous haunting.

A Piece of Everything

I walk over the discarded skin
of the world

the tree keeps falling while
it stands

I walk on myself and millions

sunlight seems to waver

everyday I hold a piece
of everything

insect dust, guano, a feather

my own ashes
awaiting

The Vertigo Blues

My aura quivers with fall. The maple's yellow paper blows
through the front door in veiny stanzas like ink crackling.
What is true? The camellia opens its white heart slowly. I wear
these blues like spread-out night. All pianists talk to their keys.

I disturb skinks with water. The oboist dances on a
column of air. There's something shivery at the threshold.
A saxophone edges out tracks inside the machine.
The old dog brushes the passage next door. Outside
a phone rings 'hello' in Jay-Z or Wolfmother, something
from Brahms that won't let me sleep. The world is loose.
Ghosts are barking, even cats shimmer.

The stage is set for rain, but sky shakes the blood, shakes
every note. And thought, that diamond, has again
been released. Yet, all my bent cheques, the sanity
of white tea, my unused sleep, my lost amulets, have not
been wasted. What makes it so difficult is also what
keeps me here, still. There are silhouettes above
my heart, a brace of baggy riffs two-timing below.

In the shining trumpet of night rain, I realize this climb
will get harder and harder and not like heaven, that
it's benign to fall. How it seems, is how it happens. How
earth moves. All is so beautiful and shifting terribly.

Unhappy Fortune

1. Unhappy

That they sealed up the doors and would not
let us forth. The external world could take care
of itself. Something was tugging, just like insects.
The overgrown metropolis was pulseless. Each day
was something missing as speech fell through
holes. Commerce had ceased. We didn't know
    how it all worked.

How can we hasten in an open that queries exchange?
All resort for ambition or pleasure was cut off — the streets
were grass-grown. Sky would spin ever so slowly, paths
picked out in all the between-ness that would sing. The city
stared itself forever, all its fuzzy little points,
the water's deep forget. Dreams caught in mangroves,
    repairs, gangways.

There were other pains, old ones you thought excised,
the suburban dark keeping to its story. That the trains
stuttered. Small toys cluttered the boxes along with
old believers. There were 101 rendezvous we never made.
That wasn't a wound nor a direct statement. There was
too much we never really had. The price of junk mail.
The embroidery on our predatoriness, a dalliance with
    ten thousand songs saved on the soft drive.

Scammers were hoping that we'd let our guard down,
the rumour of this new presence having spread itself
whisperingly around. It's true that locking up the doors
of people's houses looked very hard and cruel.
The giddiest grew pale and the more aged and sedate
passed their hands over their brows as if in reverie
    or meditation.

For so long we'd nestled in the interzone. It was
full of folds. We needed some exercise. Sometimes
the night needed rescuing from itself. Bliss
was still advertised on the rolling screens.
Cold inhabited our guts. A rescue chorus
    hung from the line.

There were the orders: the Streets to be kept Clean.
'Do not provide your personal, banking or
superannuation details to strangers who have
approached you. Seal up the doors.' Where
the infectious pestilence did reign our risk is common,
our precautions and exertions shall be common
also. 'Stay 1.5 metres away from others.' A plague is
a formidable enemy, and is armed with terrors. If there
were sharp pains, and sudden dizziness, with dissolution.
    'Throw the tissue in the bin.'

And thus were produced a multitude of gaudy and fantastic
appearances. There was much of the beautiful, much
of the wanton, much of the bizarre, something of
the terrible. 'Care to be had of unwholesome Fish
or Flesh, and of musty Corn. You can also get
up-to-date Information on the Government's
    WhatsApp channel.'

Dreams are stiff-frozen as they stand. A promise
as quick as youth, the insouciance of languages
between aisles and ring tones. It was said to be the remains
of the old animosities, which had so lately involved us all
    in blood and disorder.

2. Fortune

There's no stillness to be had. I would walk barefoot
    through the world, to find an uninfected spot.
I would build my home on some wave-tossed plank,
    drifted about on the barren, shoreless ocean.

I've dreamed of traces where old hulks lean
    into the sand, where in the wake of dunes
vegetation spreads its fingers, and in the wind
    you must hold on.

Sometimes I stand here as though no help is coming
    despite the yellow thready dawn.
Sadness begins upon boulevards
    where glass towers needle the gothic dark.

The quotidian radio sings a universal language.
    'Someone out there?'

Or I return to words that kin to breath—
    the striped shadows.

Day Shifts

Look down —
    grains & flitter
junk from spring rains

    Brilliance!
In the lateness —
every hour retreats

More leaves on the floor
& smells — sap or pollen

    The sun's still there!
Shiny glass
— falls in the room

    Not like rain
Not always to plan

    Night will be
like day — almost.
But evanescent!

In these shiftings
— estimates of rain
    & something unexpected

which isn't sorrow

To enter / As you enter / Entrances

Midway though the journey of our life
I found myself within a dark forest,
For the straight path had been lost.
—Dante

Paradise haunts gardens, and it haunts mine.
—Derek Jarman

Come slowly – Eden! ... lost in Balms
—Emily Dickinson

1. What do the plants say? The grass that moves with the wind. Is the poem the same as sex, or love, or loving? Or dying? Come into the garden and see.

2. And words are made in the body and are made from air. Consider how the anthology of your body has become. Touch it and sing it, *'the alfresco fuck is the original fuck'.*

Derek Jarman

3. How do you create a space for the living and the dying? A space for happiness and the ardent, or the cruel or sad—*'a green thought in a green shade'* or *'binding with briars my thoughts and desires'.*

Andrew Marvell; William Blake

4. Like a poem made from fragments
   what blows in
   another kind of Eden
   a body of dust shit
   the compost of the living

the chemical memory of the dead

5. The garden is a lyric. It's an epic. It tells and it shows, through its seasons. It's not a lesson nor an archetype.

6. *'Poetry began / with rhythms of rice planting / in the heart of the country'*

Matsuo Bashō

7. *'Nature is not natural, and that is natural enough.'*

Gertrude Stein

8. Let your papers and books rot in the garden, the words becoming something else, more as well as less. Add more words to the mulch. The ink, maybe, should not be there. But there's no nature here, the garden's full of plastic now. We're all filled with plastic now, shiny gleaming people, never quite destructible now. The complicity is real even as it gives you a headache. The plastic is ecstatic, as it pours from the factories. Breathe it in as you swipe your cards. Remember it.

9. *'All fixed, fast-frozen relations, with their train of ancient and venerable prejudices and opinions, are swept away'*

Marx and Engels

10. *'give some supportance to the bending twigs'*

Shakespeare

11.
'Saturday 6 [May]

Three days of a May heatwave – the greenhouse effect sets in. Dungeness is to disappear in 100 years' time beneath the waves along with its power station – which, it's said, will take 100 years to dismantle. A meteor passes close to the earth, and the ozone hole shifts over southern Australia.'

Derek Jarman

12. All writing is fragment. What do fragments sound like? How do they grow to gather? Are they melancholy fragments? *'A gorgeous dew pours down, and the roses bloom, so does tender chervil and the honey-flowering clover, and often as she wanders, she remembers ...'*

Sappho

13. A garden is a gap. Fill it with gaps. And pleasures in the gaps. All gaps fill pleasures and pleasures are gaps. And gasps. Things to grasp. Bodily sensations, fucking feelings. *Les fleurs du mal.*

Charles Baudelaire

14. A rhizome a rose. The name of the rose is another rose is another.

15. *'I could scrape the colour
   from the petals
   like spilt dye from a rock.'*

H.D.

16. You cannot make a garden but you can gather, like Varda's gleaners. You are not saving anything but you can see the shapes of detritus. Think about how you see and feel your garbage. The left of others.

17. *'the vegetal world also teaches us that we cannot continue being alive without becoming.'*

Luce Irigaray

18. The body is open. It's not an enclosure A garden never closes nor does a poem. Love what is left. Find the best place for it.

19. *'There are no walls or fences. My garden's boundaries are the horizon'*

Derek Jarman

20. The garden does not equal silence. *SILENCE=DEATH*

The Silence=Death Project

Light Falling West

I come with leaves
I swallow sunlight and hope it may cure something

I count rain as it drops past me into another eon
I enter a dream world as if I'll emerge

I rise up from the bed clothes, the ones I'll die in
I stand in my own dust that tastes of light falling west

Symposium of the Unfinished

And Random

> *I can only circle ...* —Roland Barthes

Out walking I see
a circle of ants
dispersing and joining

it looks purposeful
and random
like rain or infection

like whatever I might
call agitation
for this word or that

to join or scatter

—

How I Move

> *the project repeats me the project incompletes me*
> —Fred Moten

The body the performer
reciting its own typos
its illegibility as movement
juggling amazements

—

That Smell on the Skin

> *Desire moves. Eros is a verb.*
> *— Anne Carson*

the ancient palimpsest
that GPS I smell you like a memory

I remember when
ever I see you shadow or bright

and memory feeds the skin the page
never spotless and always hungry

—

The New Loss

> *feeding the pages to the flame*
> *—Bhanu Kapil*

Burning the skin the page
the inky stench the courage
of it as well to dissolve
in air and after ash
the loss in the ground is new

—

Dis Like

> *I, too, dislike it.*
> *—Marianne Moore*

Contempt is as genuine
as any other art
and sometimes more true

like a canker an itch
a need

—

Faltering

> *a feeble shadow of an original conception*
> *—Ben Lerner*

Sad as breakfast
or an empty train
rattle of technology
faltering
in the loaded quantum
of autumn air
echo of a crowd
across the bare oval

—

Around the Genuine

> *Meaning is more of a dance*
> —Nuar Alsadir

The curve of a bowl
breaking
or a street a hand
letting go
the way life contracts
to a room
or rises over the world
with wings or bombs
satellite eclipse
sung in the static

the next day and
the next are unfinished
sentences looking
like rain in syllables
ash unsettles
walking a circle around
the genuine the faltering

unfinis rememb amazem
eclips

the body betrays what it loves
by saying it loves its betrayals

Between Here and the Underworld

I am an answer, I am a question, as if I was
the god's favourite. I'm the left hand, struck
blind to see, struck with age and breasts. I'm this sex
which is, is not, in all my tender clothing. I was
a book, maybe still am, a bit turned or stained
by fingers, or the sun, as I'm hunting my text for
the wild irregular. I'm a vindication of darkness, I'm
this button which is not one.

I'm wrinkled time, born in the sick house.
I could hear evening on its way, I was the present tense,
younger than anyone for a split-second, fresh-ancient
storm-red, closing on Khaos, mother night. I'm still
dancing myself whole, in cursing loneliness, in the
forgetting of wisdom, still hungry, on the hunt
and bedevilled.

I'm living between here and the underworld, or
leaning out of the window reflecting on existence,
still hearing the birds, their omens in my backyard under
that hole in the sky. I'm living with ten parts of love
in one body, present and future, dust and bread. What
did I learn as a woman? Or a man, the man
I had to be, to be invisible.

I'm often parallel to myself or to you. If I say
'I'll see you in hell, or in heaven' I will, of course. Or
in the corridor as we pass, where I'm jaunty under
the circumstances, a wager of dissidence
and beer. Or I'm in the mood for love,
perhaps, perhaps, an echo of night, where things
rise and tumble.

I'm still on my feet, holding out for all those
stained future tenses. Here are my arms, this body which
is, is not, in all its wild and cursive hunger.

Still, Life

light glazes evening   graffiti shade   hissbike
shivergrass   cement lawn   a muddling breeze
a man stands at a bus stop wiping his face with his right hand

a path of castoffs   deserted hairclip   yellchild
mulchcrackle   L plate   the tolling of crossings
there's the distant sound of an ambulance

announcements without bodies   empty train   dogpuff
crowsight   'Total Eclipse …'   blue tape on a pole
a pink kid's sunhat hanging from a letterbox

the buzzing of autumn lawns
still, life

21 March – 12 April 2020

Everything comes – at first glance

I heard a fly buzz and then a blue
uncertain advent, an hallucinatory relish
tasting a lot like today's weather
and how everything has shifted
into pieces of rain, the muffled
cloudy light, then the precarious
held infinitude, thunder outside
the stillness in the room

This is my undercover, dubious
atopic, the dream of reading
on the bed, the tattoo of words
is sticky, adjectives like incandescent
metal, phrases wrung with boredom
as well as ripening, the verbs full
of hackles, the erotic colour of
scandal and fictions

Boredom is my alibi as I trace lines
around zero yet with delicacy
that taste of libidinal devotion, an agent
of contagion, as the air smells
of violets, orris root, and recalls
the iris of the garden we lost
but still here in this potpourri of phrases
love potions, the tincture of transport

With what portion of me be, I thank
this bliss for reminding me
of fecondité and transmutation out of
a sentence, o jubilation, o apostrophe
ejaculation! beyond, see!
every housewifely bird picking up
what it needs between the heaves of storm
under the intransitive air

'I only wanted to see what the garden was like'

Whether slovenly or splendid
I'm leaning into
the darkness yet again

As if I was a disbanded girl
whose lucid life
was called inside

My smashed vision
misses everything
but the detours and shade

How should I make
myself different
With an identity pass
or redactions

I have boxes of medicine
for everything
flowers of sulphur and restoratives
amphetamine lip balm

I tremor before reality
I have no electronic desire

I spend an hour staring
at a verb
It stares back
It knows I'm fraudulent

I think about my dreams
of mutiny
and burn the poems

I have this old memory
of objects on a table
a blind mirror, a severe dark rose
a cruel figurine
Who will explain them to me

Or how to re-enter the world
in the morning
as a child in the garden
unreachable and endless

I'm Almost Good

My goddess part has deserted me, though I watch stars
over my shoulder. It makes me dizzy.

My heart's white as copy paper
waiting for my next lie.

My bones are almost as tired as my skin.
My skin is too tight to think.

I am half-elegy, and half-chewed sweet.

I collect dust but only certain dust.
No, I won't tell you that secret.

I wake when I sleep
and don't know where I am.

This is normal.

I disposed of some junk. I talked through something epic.
Really, it seemed almost good.

I'm skirting the hours. I can't put anything into them.
I can't grasp even the seams of minutes.

I could walk over myself, if I wasn't so tired.

But I look as though I'm meant to be here
doing something important.

I don't need anyone's permission
to speculate that something's breaking.

I know everything is woe
and there's loud carriage in my head.

The timetable almost clicks into place.
The stories almost sound true and present.

Still, outside the window a honeyeater sings.
So does the city's traffic.

Above, there's a pressure of clouds
pretending to a storm front.

No-one's fooling anyone.
It's tense, it's not great.

No wonder I lean on the fence
as if it's the place to be.

Here's the gate, there's the road.
And now the rain, the wet ground. That pitch!

Really, it seems almost good.

Here We Are

thin silver wind   in eucalypts
dust the precious   drowsy sweetness
yellow in open morning turn
to autumn   magpie, kookaburra
corella, pigeon   even in bird rage
for territory   sweets in windowed air
every minute   o that remarkable
what would nectar do   o you angles
of dawn, breasting dawn   o seriously
feathers out there   150 million kilometres
of light   o sunspot activity   Asian cyclones
o melting Antarctica   here we are
openings in sea   fissures in the electric
the dream in wake   on walls the big dance
shadow thick night sings   bye-bye-bye
o breath, I and you breath   then breathe
this shadow wake for the not numbed
o let me stretch forth for another
and it comes into me   this day like
this day   what's not wrong is not wrong
and round the room   high in the aerials
every digital wing   what sing!
dream carcass empties   sleepless empties
sorry worry empties   here full
the blast of traffic into a space
o glittery space   fleet thin silver
immense 150 million gold   waving oxygen
to taste   and to tempt
this kiss welcome here   my skin
here my walk again   here I am
a part   and who is that flickering the door
parcels of dust and making   footsteps
making more dust   in every
clever molecule   all the leaves are grey
so   they shine

Future Shadow

> *'When we try to pick out anything by itself, we find it hitched to everything else in the Universe.'*
>
> – *John Muir,* My First Summer in the Sierra

Song 1

Let's sing the remaining songs
those that still curve through us
those tasting of something
yet solid, songs of rice and bread.

Let's hope they'll move us
like earth and beaches, whisky,
daylight moons, gulls, magpies,
nimbus clouds, old wharves.

And let them swim in our throats
open and close like a great choir
of air, let its archaic winds blow
against our faces as we taste old dust,
eucalypt, pine and ash, rose,
bottlebrush, jasmine, palm and grass.

*

and I was out on the grass, as breathreek, mulchchamber
snakes whispered in my ear, 'how much time do we have'

*

Divination 1

3am glows
next to you
   you should tremble
but you simply reach
for that light
   from another world

the one thing
it doesn't promise
   is peace

(somewhere
the dark's regained
   but never named)

*

as if god never left nor arrived, as if beauty wasn't yet a word
colours just the way light was on our eyes

*

Divination 2

'sky
  no longer
  blue
out of blackness
  steadily
  pale white stars
overhead
  motionless hull
  the huge red sun
salt ocean
  all bloody
  under eternal sunset'

When I talk to myself
I don't hear myself
Well, I hear my breath, and my heart
in my ears (so much these days)

I taste myself, a little sweetness round my teeth
I may smell of apples or phlegm
coffee and the heat on my skin

I see the map on my hand
Maybe it's all a warning
Who knows what happens next?
Is there something to talk about again?
Does the sunset find me angry?

*

I taste the old gall in ink, between the page, the garden, the sea.

*

Divination 3

I stand by the shore under the ancient sun
as a plastic bag rolls in. I scoop it up and bin it.
As if that does any good.

Researchers are making heart valves
out of plastics supple enough to simulate
opening and closing.
The caterpillar of *Galleria mellonella*
eats plastic garbage.
As polyethylene burns it gives off
the smell of paraffin. It continues burning
after the flame is removed.

Yes, we know a smog of microplastic circles
through the ocean's gyres, algae, and fish guts.
It's hard to remember what it was once like.
In the chain reaction of things, our hearts
keep missing their beats.

*

'What if my leaves are falling
   O bright locks of the approaching storm.'

*

          molecules
                    matter

*

A damaged present
its pulse: 'delete your account'
'do you take requests?'   'I'm not selling solutions'

in a station a fly   buzzes

streets   names
oceans of plastic waste land

~~a rose is a rose is a rose~~

I don't have to
change my life
life changes me
within me

*

'Scatter ashes and sparks ... if winter comes.'

    'All fall down
        All fall down'

*

Divination 4

'vast and irregular
  plains of ice
  lost among
  the distant inequalities
  lost in
  distance'

*

Like the torn
I saw how winter
or how spring

I saw how damage

'oozy woods, sapless foliage
  grey with fear'

I tore this coat
the fabric's holes

I grab this coat
that doesn't fit

A home is
what you leave

*

The Oracle says: 'Pray to the Winds.'

*

In reeds and dark
how many poems about
dying can I write? By what right?
The underworld has nothing
to teach me yet

I'm no queen of any world
I'm simply part of the commons
where all remains remain

the gutter, the sewer, the course
caught up or stagnant or overflowing
in a cloak of reeds and dark

*

        that   resonance
        god in matter   ghostly   bones
        (have you forgotten?)   the wind   an angel
        clammy with passion
        exits become dawn

*

A Plea

I think about walking as something to do
Each moment is an event in some kind of light

Why is the tree broken, the other beautiful
the sky is all over the place

The joinery of the day is clanking in a truck

Whether light is crepuscular or rosy-fingered
it's never sorry, or wrong

Sometimes I'm frightened by hedges
Hold my hand when it gets even scarier

*

'We brought nothing into this world, and it is certain we can carry
    nothing out.'

*

Song 2

Let's sing of unknownings.
Maybe they'll open up like our pores
our gills, our fibre, our wings
through old centuries of ink and blood
the pulp of pages, pulp of a heart
crying and sweat.

*

       whatever you wish   it sticks to you
          becomes
      quiet   perfect   daybreak

*

I come with leaves and sap, I come with
continuous breath, to the abundant end of the day

*

Watching for daybreak
when all that is   rises and returns
fine dust   molecules   resonances   cold clouds

every god in its matter looks like whatever you wish
dogs return with wolf sounds   and ghostly bones
all the fine plants hang from your lips or scalp

have you wandered so far
you've forgotten where you've come from

the wind's like an angel   it sticks to you
   the stairs become clammy with passionate sweat

let me take you to a place where gods are born
    between eventide and thighs   under covers or near exits
a place that becomes a quiet night   a perfect end

or watching for daybreak
   light floods
      then yields

*

Divination 5

'clear as a fresh wind blowing
   against the sun's uprising ...
   What is to come, will come.'

*

'Winged seeds, the dreaming earth, living hues, moving everywhere.'

Dark Heart

When dark is drawn
in every thing
a tooth of every mask
knot of every manacle

Each plan is dark
in outline, in the end
you fail, as sunshine
fails its dream

Walk into the sea
as though it is
the end of the narrative
pull the water over you

We are all targets
we all hunt the world

Darling Sense

Each day rising with you
is my way of salvage
out of the present's dire,
it's coercive bigness.

We turn here on a plain
among the crescendo of more
where new conceptions
suck out ancient sequences
to render receivers, trackers,
buttons that clutch up nothing
in this darkling.

We're not mothers nor are we
immaculate. We're meant to be
the nurturing kind, but it's hard
to be kind.

Still, we wire into each
other's curves or the moon
but even our breathing
seems to warm
the world too much.

Perhaps we can sister things.
It may not match
the diligence that's fitting
but we yes, and stress
for the world we're in,
not claim, not over-tread.

We don't need to hold on things
to liven with them more, just to
do, just to do in ordinary

benevolence
as our hands come
to hand.

There are other crescendos, things
no-one need know,
how we preserve our ample
bracing, freshen
our private measures,
turn heat to
its darling sense.

Undo Everything

I resurrect the dead for a second when I close my eyes.
It's hard to remember what it was once like.
I look at each plant for belief or breath.

    Sorrow isn't something I'd name.

Knots are possibilities. I weave them
out of themselves, tenderly, curiously, like a charm.
There are cold things I can't brush away.

    Hold my hand when it gets even scarier.

I remember the taste of water.
Sky's beautiful dry shadows fall on my pages
through the familiar spectrum.

    Even the yellow door is sighing.

I taste the old gall in ink, between the page,
the garden, the sea. I collect dust but only certain dust.
I taste myself, apples or phlegm, the heat on my skin.

    I ask emptiness to fill me.

The body betrays what it loves by saying it loves
its betrayals, reciting its own typos, juggling amazements
as if god never left nor arrived.

    Everything hurts, so, maybe that's the case.

Boredom is my alibi as I trace lines around zero.
But I look as though I'm meant to be here
doing something important.

    Really, it seems almost good.

I have boxes of medicine for everything. I think about
my dreams of mutiny and burn the poems.
I'm leaning into the darkness yet again.

    I think about walking as something to do.

The natural state is turning, as if there was more space
in the continuum. I see you shadow or bright.
In these shiftings   something unexpected

    which isn't sorrow.

Wild Curious Air

I walk through the curious air.
   I feel earth thrust and scrape.

Each plant breath
   unveils me as shadow guest
in the wild space of afternoon.

All shadows have their own colours.
The next day and the next
   are unfinished.

Let's stride out anyway
   fresh-ancient   mortal

Afterword

Wild Curious Air is a conversation, a series of readings or observances, or a kind of symposium, as it speaks both to itself and through itself to other works. It is part of my ongoing concern with composition as a dismantling or recomposing of boundaries, and ways of writing/reading. Words and phrases by other writers are, therefore, integral parts of some of the poems here. This is a kind of reading with or alongside other texts and genres, as well as a walking with, rather than any forced notion of collaboration.

The idea of walking also exists in the book as an ecological practice, an attention to specific places and placing. 'Attention is a register', to quote one of the poems: attention as it registers as language on the page and in the ear, as well as a register of tone, range or level of feeling, and also as an accounting, a testing both through language and in the body.

It is also a book of shiftings, of moving among texts, or as language being written by acting in the world. The shiftings are of ideas, words, and bodies, through curiosity, breath and breathlessness, intimacies and desires, ecstatic, dreaming or vertiginous states, the ever-presence of death in life, a sense of observance or ritual, and continuous retrievals of memory. As well as any other shiftings a reader may care to find, as there are always effects beyond a poet's intentions or ambitions despite their stated practice, including those this Afterword is proposing. Nonetheless, some of these states are personally embodied; they're a part of how I work, sometimes unconsciously but also in ways I'm very aware of as I write.

Finally, it is a book of play (in the most expansive sense of that term) and pleasure that also acknowledges the global emergencies of the 21st century, and the book registers directly or by implication some of those states or events. Words such as 'light' and 'night' recur in near equal measure throughout the book. In other words, the diurnal, daily ongoingness, is central, both formally and as affect. It is a calling to, a calling up of many small, close and distant, big things made in language, made as moving among and through the things of this world.

Notes on Poems

'The Moon, Antares, and the Dead As Well': The epigraph and the quoted phrase in the poem are from John Berger, *and our faces, my heart, brief as photos*. The poem owes something to a reading of parts of Berger's book.

'It doesn't hurt to fall off the moon': The poem's title quotes dialogue from the Jacques Rivette film, *Céline et Julie vont en bateau: Phantom Ladies Over Paris (Celine and Julie Go Boating)*.

'Unhappy Fortune': Includes texts (and distortions of those texts) from *Romeo and Juliet*, William Shakespeare (including the poem's title); *A Journal of the Plague Year*, Daniel Defoe; *The Masque of the Red Death*, Edgar Allan Poe; *The Last Man*, Mary Shelley; ACCC (Australian Competition and Consumer Commission) Scamwatch website; Australian Government Department of Health website.

'To enter/As you enter/Entrances': 'Midway though the journey ...', Dante, *Inferno*; 'Paradise haunts gardens ...', Derek Jarman, *Modern Nature*; 'Come slowly ...', Emily Dickinson; 'the alfresco fuck ...' Derek Jarman, *Modern Nature*; 'a green thought ...', Andrew Marvell 'The Garden'; 'binding with briars ...', William Blake, 'The Garden of Love'; 'Poetry began ...', my version of Bashō's poem beginning 'fūryū no ...'; 'Nature is not natural, ...' Gertrude Stein, *Ida: A Novel*; 'All fixed, fast-frozen relations...' Marx and Engels, *The Communist Manifesto*; 'give some supportance ...', Shakespeare, *Richard II*; 'Saturday 6 [May]', Derek Jarman, *Modern Nature*; 'A gorgeous dew ...' Sappho *Fr.96* (my rendering using various translations); 'I could scrape the colour ...', HD, *The Garden*; 'the vegetal world ...' Luce Irigaray, 'What the Vegetal World Says to Us' in *The Language of Plants: Science, Philosophy, Literature*, eds Monica Gagliano, Patricia Vieira, & John Charles Ryan; 'There are no walls ...', Derek Jarman, *Modern Nature*; 'SILENCE=DEATH', The Silence=Death Project, founded during the AIDS crisis, and most known for the poster using these words: a six-person collective consisting of Avram Finkelstein, Brian Howard, Oliver Johnston, Charles Kreloff, Chris Lione, and Jorge Soccarás.

'Symposium of the Unfinished': The epigraphs to each section are from, in order: *The Pleasure of the Text*, Roland Barthes; 'The Gramsci Monument', Fred Moten; *Eros the Bittersweet*, Anne Carson; 'Avert the Icy Feeling', Bhanu Kapil; 'Poetry', Marianne Moore; *The Hatred of Poetry*, Ben Lerner; 'Quantum Displacement', Nuar Alsadir.

'Between Here and the Underworld': The poem alludes to a number of book titles, including *The Left Hand of Darkness*, Ursula Le Guin; *This Sex Which is Not One (Ce sexe qui n'en est pas un)*, Luce Irigaray; *Tender Buttons*, Gertrude Stein; *Hunting the Wild Pineapple*, Thea Astley; *The Present Tense*, Gwen Harwood; *A Vindication of the Rights of Woman*, Mary Wollstonecraft; *A Wrinkle in Time*, Madeleine L'Engle; *The Well of Loneliness*, Radclyffe Hall; *The Getting of Wisdom*, Henry Handel Richardson; as well as films by Roy Andersson, *A Pigeon Sat on a Branch Reflecting on Existence*, and Wong Kar-wai, *In the Mood For Love*.

'Everything comes – at first glance': Contains a number of words and a few phrases from 'I heard a Fly buzz' by Emily Dickinson, and the English translation of *The Pleasure of the Text* by Roland Barthes, including the poem's title.

'I only wanted to see what the garden was like': The poem's title quotes from *Through the Looking Glass, and What Alice Found There,* by Lewis Carroll. The poem itself was written after watching a documentary about Alejandra Pizarnick entitled *Alejandra* (dir. Ernesto Ardito, Virna Molina), and refers indirectly to some of Pizarnik's poems and other writings.

'Future Shadow': All words in quote marks are taken from the following: 'Divination 2': from *The Time Machine*, H.G. Wells.; 'What if my leaves ...': words and phrases collaged from Shelley's 'Ode to the West Wind'; 'Scatter ashes and sparks ...': words and phrases collaged from Shelley's 'Ode to the West Wind', and the nursery rhyme 'Ring a Ring o' Rosie'; 'Divination 4': from *Frankenstein*, Mary Shelley; 'oozy woods ...': words and phrases collaged from Shelley's 'Ode to the West Wind'; 'Pray to the winds': the Delphic Oracle's advice to the Delphians prior to the Battle of Salamis, *The History of Herodotus, Book VII, 178* (trs GC Macaulay); 'We brought nothing into this world, ...': 1 Tim. 6:7, also 'At the Burial of the Dead', *The Book of Common Prayer*; 'a quiet night ... a perfect end': from 'The Order For Compline', *The Book of Common Prayer*; 'Divination 5': from Cassandra's speech in Aeschylus' *Agamemnon*; 'Winged seeds ...': words and phrases collaged from Shelley's 'Ode to the West Wind'. There are also brief references and/or gestures to poems by Ezra Pound, Emily Dickinson, Gertrude Stein, and Rainer Maria Rilke, and an allusion to a song by the Pet Shop Boys. 'Does the sunset find me angry?' is a reference to Eph 4:26, also part of *The Order For Compline*.

Acknowledgements

Some of the poems in this book were first published in various print or online periodicals and anthologies, sometimes in different forms. My thanks to the various editors of: *The Australian; Communion; Hecate; Journal of Poetics Research; Meanjin; Not Very Quiet; Otoliths; Shearsman (UK)*.

'The Vertigo Blues' appeared in *The Quality of Light and other poems*, Garron Press, Adelaide, 2017.

'Last Small Things' first appeared in *No News: 90 Poets Reflect on a Unique BBC Newscast*, edited by Paul Munden, Alvin Pang and Shane Strange, Recent Work Press, 2020.

About the Author

Jill Jones was born in Sydney and has lived in Adelaide since 2008. Recent books include *A History Of What I'll Become*, *Viva the Real*, which was shortlisted for the 2019 Prime Minister's Literary Awards for Poetry and the 2020 John Bray Award, and *Brink*. In 2015 she won the Victorian Premier's Prize for Poetry for *The Beautiful Anxiety*. Her work is represented in a number of major anthologies including *The Macquarie PEN Anthology of Australian Literature*, *Contemporary Australian Poetry*, and *The Penguin Anthology of Australian Poetry*. She is a member of the J.M. Coetzee Centre for Creative Practice, University of Adelaide, where she teaches creative writing and literary studies. Prior to her career as an academic, she was a film reviewer, journalist, book editor, and arts administrator. In late 2014 she was poet-in-residence at Stockholm University. Her work has been translated into Chinese, French, Italian, Czech, Macedonian and Spanish.

www.ingramcontent.com/pod-product-compliance
Lightning Source LLC
Chambersburg PA
CBHW020330010526
44107CB00054B/2054